For the Graduate

For the Graduate

Felicia Wiggins

Illustrated by Eliza Gran

Ariel Books

Andrews McMeel Publishing

Kansas City

 For information write Andrews McMeel Publishing, an Andrews McMeel Universal company, 4520 Main Street, Kansas City, Missouri 64111.

www.andrewsmcmeel.com

Book Design by Junie Lee

ISBN: 0-8362-6989-6
Library of Congress Catalog Card Number: 98-84949

Contents

Introduction

Graduation Day . . . finally. You *have* arrived. You are now at a fulfilling yet challenging crossroads in your life. There is much you may feel nostalgic for—an irreplaceable classmate, a special or even dreaded teacher, late-night study sessions, perhaps your favorite extracurricular activities. Above all, you won't soon forget all the years of hard work that made this day possible.

Introduction

You knew you had it in you! This is a tribute to your success and a wish for continuing achievement as a student of the world. Congratulations, graduate, on a job well done!

Good-bye

School Days

A love affair with knowledge will never end in heartbreak.

-Michael Garrett Marino

A one-book man is either a slow learner or an ill-equipped teacher.

-Robert William Burke

What is research, but a blind date with knowledge?

–Will Henry

Sometimes a scream is better than a thesis.

–Ralph Waldo Emerson

One's work may be finished some day, but one's education never.

–Alexandre Dumas

A good education should leave much to be desired.

–Alan Gregg

The children need the bread of the mind.

–Rafael Cordero y Molina

Soap and education are not as sudden as a massacre, but they are more deadly in the long run.

-Mark Twain

Better build schoolrooms for
“the boy,”
Than cells and gibbets for “the man.”

-Eliza Cook

The proper study of mankind is books.

–Aldous Huxley

If someone had told me I would be pope one day, I would have studied harder.

–Pope John Paul I

Schoolmasters and parents exist to be grown out of.

-John Wolfenden

Nothing in education is so astonishing as the amount of ignorance it accumulates in the form of inert facts.

-Henry Adams

I have never let my schooling interfere with my education.

-Mark Twain

My education was the liberty I had to read indiscriminately and all the time, with my eyes hanging out.

–Dylan Thomas

Some books are meant to be tasted, others to be swallowed, and some few to be chewed and digested.

-Francis Bacon

Sweet
Success

Give to the world the best you have
and the best will come back to you.

-Madeline Bridges

Success is the result of perfection, hard work, learning from failure, loyalty, and persistence.

-Colin Powell

It takes time to be a success, but time is all it takes.

-Anonymous

Act as if it were impossible to fail.

-Dorothea Brande

I have not failed. I've just found ten thousand ways that won't work.

-Thomas Alva Edison

If there is no dull and determined effort, there will be no brilliant achievement.

-Hsun-tzu

Success is going from failure to failure without loss of enthusiasm.

-Sir Winston Churchill

A first-rate soup is better than a second-rate painting.

-Abraham Lincoln

You can't sustain success on a gimmick and no talent.

–Sade

Do it big or stay in bed.

–Larry Kelly

I have learned that success is to be measured not so much by the position that one has reached in life as by the obstacles which he has overcome while trying to succeed.

-Booker T. Washington

To tend, unfailingly, unflinchingly, toward a goal, is the secret of success.

-Anna Pavlova

If at first you don't succeed, you're running about average.

–M. H. Alderson

You always pass failure on the way to success.

–Mickey Rooney

Success seems to be largely a matter of hanging on after others have let go.

-William Feather

If at first you don't succeed, try, try, try again.

-W. E. Hickson

Success produces success, just as money produces money.

-Nicolas de Chamfort

Success is not the result of spontaneous combustion. You must set yourself on fire.

-Reggie Leach

Ask yourself the secret of *your* success. Listen to your answer, and practice it.

–Richard Bach

Daring Does It

Success often comes to those who dare and act; it seldom goes to the timid who are ever afraid of the consequences.

-Jawaharlal Nehru

Take risks: If you win, you will be happy; if you lose, you will be wise.

-Anonymous

It is impossible to win the great prizes of life without running risks.

–Theodore Roosevelt

Our doubts are traitors, and make us lose the good we oft might win. . . .

–William Shakespeare

My passions were all gathered together like fingers that made a fist. Drive is considered aggression today; I knew it then as purpose.

-Bette Davis

They say you can't do it, but sometimes it doesn't always work.

-Casey Stengel

Ah, but a man's reach should exceed his grasp, or what's a heaven for?

–Robert Browning

Winning isn't everything, but wanting to win is.

–Vince Lombardi

Mama exhorted her children at every opportunity to "jump at de sun." We might not land on the sun, but at least we would get off the ground.

-Zora Neale Hurston

Seize opportunity by the beard, for it is bald behind.

-Bulgarian proverb

Your Hard Work

A = X

If A is a success in life, then A equals x plus y plus z. Work is x; y is play; and z is keeping your mouth shut.

-Albert Einstein

Work is much more fun than fun.

-Noel Coward

The only place where success comes before work is a dictionary.

-Vidal Sassoon

Enthusiasm for one's goal lessens the disagreeableness of working toward it.

-Thomas Eakins

To travel hopefully is a better thing than to arrive, and the true success is to labor.

-Robert Louis Stevenson

If all the year were playing holidays,
To sport would be as tedious as to
work. . . .

-William Shakespeare

If a man wants his dream to come true, he must wake up.

-Anonymous

I am not the smartest or most talented person in the world, but I succeeded because I keep going, and going, and going.

-Sylvester Stallone

Nothing to do but work,
Nothing to eat but food,
Nothing to wear but clothes
To keep one from going nude.

-Benjamin Franklin King

When the going gets tough, the tough get going.

-Joseph P. Kennedy

It ain't over 'til it's over.

-Yogi Berra

I know the price of success: dedication, hard work, and an unremitting devotion to the things you want to see happen.

-Frank Lloyd Wright

You can have unbelievable intelligence, you can have connections, you can have opportunities fall out of the sky. But in the end, hard work is the true, enduring characteristic of successful people.

-Marsha Evans

Big shots are only little shots who kept shooting.

–Christopher Morley

Striving for success without hard work is like trying to harvest where you haven't planted.

–David Bly

A man can make what he wants of himself if he truly believes that he must be ready for hard work and many heartbreaks along the way.

-Thurgood Marshall

God helps them that help themselves.

-Benjamin Franklin

We must live like angels and produce like the devil!

—Luis Muñoz Marín

The man who does just enough work to get by seldom gets more than "by."

-Samuel B. Fuller

The world stands aside to let anyone pass who knows where he is going.

-David Starr Jordan